Developmental Editing for Fiction

Sophie Playle

First published in the UK in 2022 by
Chartered Institute of Editing and Proofreading
Apsley House
176 Upper Richmond Road
London
SW15 2SH

ciep.uk

Copyright © 2022 Chartered Institute of Editing and Proofreading

ISBN 978 1 915141 10 1 (print)
ISBN 978 1 915141 11 8 (PDF ebook)

All rights reserved. No part of this publication may be reproduced or used in any manner without written permission from the publisher, except for quoting brief passages in a review.

The moral rights of the author have been asserted.

The information in this work is accurate and current at the time of publication to the best of the author's and publisher's knowledge, but it has been written as a short summary or introduction only. Readers are advised to take further steps to ensure the correctness, sufficiency or completeness of this information for their own purposes.

Development editing, copyediting and proofreading by CIEP members, including Julia Sandford-Cooke, Liz Dalby, Harriet Power, Abi Saffrey and Llinos Edwards.

Typeset in-house
Original design by Ave Design (**avedesignstudio.com**)
Creative commons images from Pixabay

Contents

1 |	Introduction	1
2 |	An overview of the service	3
	Developmental editing versus book coaching	3
	Understanding the author's goals	3
	Knowing the audience	4
	Assessing the script	4
	Higher-level analysis	5
	Who hires developmental fiction editors?	5
	When does developmental editing happen?	7
3 |	General principles	9
	Remember, it's not your book!	9
	Avoid overwhelming the author	9
	Provide objective feedback	10
	Understand novel-writing conventions	10
4 |	Writing-craft topics that you need to know about	13
	Story	13
	Plot	15
	Character	16
	Point of view	17
	Setting and worldbuilding	20
	Scene and summary: show and tell	21
	Genre	22
	Readership and market potential	23

5 |	Conducting a developmental edit	25
	Different approaches to feedback	25
	Gathering information	27
	Assessing and pricing projects	28
	Page notes	30
	Editorial reports/summary letters	31
	Pointers on providing feedback	32
	Book maps and summary spreadsheets	34
6 |	Next steps in becoming a developmental editor	35
	Learning and training	35
	Building experience	36
7 |	Resources	37
	Courses	37
	Books	37
	Blogs and websites	39
	Forums and communities	40

1 | Introduction

Developmental editing is very different from most other forms of editing. Typically, when we think of editing, we think of changing the text at sentence level. Developmental editing takes a more macro approach: it's concerned with helping the author develop and refine their story, and the techniques they use to tell that story.

If you love reading novels, are a voracious reader and are interested in the craft of writing, you might enjoy developmental editing. Developmental editing is a skill and service in its own right, so copyediting and proofreading experience isn't necessary to get started in this field.

Having said that, perhaps you have some experience of copyediting or proofreading fiction, and:

- found yourself advising the author on bigger storytelling aspects of their novel that stood out to you
- felt that the story could have been better, but weren't sure exactly how (or indeed how to present such feedback to them).

If either of these scenarios sounds familiar, learning more about developmental editing will allow you to expand your services to help authors improve their novels beyond the sentence level. But if you have no copyediting or proofreading experience at all, that's fine too: you can offer developmental editing alone, without copyediting or proofreading.

This guide is an introduction to developmental fiction editing. It provides:

- what you need to know in order to offer developmental editing
- an overview of the different methods of developmental editing
- ideas on how to get started.

2 | An overview of the service

Let's start by defining developmental editing. As with most editorial services, definitions can vary, but in essence:

> Developmental editing helps authors identify – and solve – the big-picture storytelling issues in a completed draft of their book. Developmental editors provide analysis and suggestions to guide authors on how they might revise their manuscripts so they have a greater chance of reaching their creative and publishing goals.

Developmental editing versus book coaching

Developmental editors usually work on completed drafts. If an author wants feedback on an incomplete draft, it's often because they're unsure of their idea and don't know how to bring everything together into a coherent story.

Helping authors finish drafting their book is more akin to book coaching, which is different from developmental editing. Book coaches work more with the author (helping them form habits and mindset, and acting as a sounding board for ideas, for example), and less with the material itself.

A book coach can help an author during multiple stages of the creative process, depending on the author's needs; they may or may not also offer developmental editing.

Understanding the author's goals

The author's creative and publishing goals inform the developmental editor's analysis of their manuscript, so it's important to ask the author about these. For example, they might want to write a fast-paced thriller with a romance subplot that doesn't end with the two main characters together. Your feedback would be based on helping them achieve this goal in the most effective and satisfying way for the reader.

Knowing the audience

Knowing who the book's readers will be is equally important. On the one hand, if the author is aiming to send their manuscript to literary agents, in the hope of being picked up by a traditional publishing house, you would be likely to advise the author on how to make their manuscript appeal to a large but specific readership.

On the other hand, if the author wants to self-publish a handful of copies to give to friends and family, and they aren't concerned about sales numbers – rather, telling their story in a specific way – it's likely you would be advising the author differently.

Assessing the script

Developmental editors assess the manuscript as a whole. If you're coming to developmental editing from a copyediting or proofreading background, you'll be used to focusing on the details. Developmental editing requires a substantial shift in perspective.

There are many components that go into a novel, and how well an author has handled each one and made them work together creates the overall reading experience. These include:

- story
- plot
- character
- point of view (POV)
- setting and worldbuilding
- and so on.

A developmental editor helps an author deconstruct and rebuild their manuscript so that all the storytelling components work together to create a better book – one that matches their goals.

Higher-level analysis

Fiction developmental editing is all about helping the author make sure the foundations of their novel are sound. Developmental editors do not fix typos or do any mechanical sentence-level editing: they don't copyedit or proofread the manuscript. The author might need to delete or rewrite large portions of their book, so any copyediting or proofreading done at this stage would be a waste of your time and effort as the editor, as well as the author's money.

Another reason that developmental editors stay clear of copyediting and proofreading is that if the editor is focusing on such minute, sentence-level issues, they can be distracted from the big-picture issues in the book. For this reason, it's important that developmental editors learn to focus the lens through which they look at the manuscript to the right depth of field.

Who hires developmental fiction editors?

Developmental editors can work with publishers or packagers, or directly with authors.

Publishers and packagers

Publishers sometimes hire developmental editors when their authors submit contracted manuscripts that they feel aren't quite up to scratch. They might also enlist the help of a developmental editor for books written by celebrities. Generally, these authors need more creative input, as writing is not their main vocation. Often, the developmental editor needs to work to a tight schedule and provide advice that addresses the most prominent, quick-to-fix issues so that the publishing schedule remains on target.

Sometimes, publishers also outsource their book production to external companies (packagers), and the packager hires a developmental editor, if needed.

Authors seeking a book deal

Authors also hire developmental editors. Literary agents and publishers are inundated with manuscript submissions: generally, it doesn't make sense for them to pay for developmental editing for brand new authors when they can simply choose the best manuscripts that come their way.

For this reason, developmental editing can be a useful service for authors aiming to be traditionally published. Although there are never any guarantees in publishing, with the help of a developmental editor authors might be able to elevate their manuscript so it has less chance of being rejected by agents and publishers.

Self-publishing authors

Developmental editing can be an extremely valuable service for self-publishing authors, too. Self-publishing (also known as independent or 'indie' publishing) is when an author uploads their novel directly to book distribution services, bypassing the need for a traditional publishing house.

There used to be a stigma around self-publishing, as many people assumed that only authors whose books were 'not good enough' to attract a traditional deal self-published. However, this is not necessarily the case. For example, LJ Ross may have self-published her crime thriller, *Holy Island*, at first because no agent picked her up, but she has now sold more than 7 million copies worldwide of all her books, and was shortlisted for a British Book Award for *Impostor* – she now has no intention of signing with a publisher.

Many authors choose to self-publish because of the creative freedom it allows them. These days, self-publishers make up a large part of the market for fiction editors, as authors have learned to commission freelance professionals to help them with quality control.

If an author were to choose to self-publish their novel, in an ideal world they would first commission a developmental edit, then a copyedit, then a proofread. Ideally, each of these services would be conducted by different people so the manuscript had as many eyes on it as possible. However, the developmental editor might also conduct the copyedit or proofread, depending on their skill set, although if they attempt all three levels of editing, there is a high chance they will miss errors due to being too familiar with the text.

In reality, self-publishing authors might not have the budget to commission all these levels of editing. Having to pay for their own quality control is one of the major pitfalls of self-publishing, and so the services commissioned by the author depend on both the needs of the manuscript, and what the author feels is most important for their book.

When does developmental editing happen?

As outlined previously, developmental editing comes before any sentence-level work. It's usually the first level of professional feedback an author receives on their manuscript.

Rough draft stage

The author might request feedback on a rough draft to help them feel more confident in spending their time and effort refining their book. Sometimes, authors want a professional to tell them whether their book has potential – again, before they spend resources working on it further.

Complete draft stage

An author might ask you to look at a draft they've pushed to the limit of their capabilities, to help them elevate their book beyond what they could achieve on their own. Often a fresh, knowledgeable perspective is invaluable here.

Beta reading

Some authors also work with beta readers. The idea of beta reading comes from the engineering concept of beta testing, which involves assessing how a product will fare in the real world, in an end-user's hands.

Beta reading works in a similar way. An author asks a small selection of people representative of their target readership to read a draft of their book, which gives the author insight into how the larger target readership might receive the novel. The beta reader tells the author what they did and didn't enjoy about the book, and their feedback is based on opinion, not analysis. Beta reading is often done for free (readers enjoy being involved in the process) or on a quid pro quo basis ('you read my novel, I'll read yours'), but some people offer it as a paid service. Generally, beta readers charge a lot less than developmental editors.

Authors usually benefit from some kind of big-picture feedback. As a developmental editor, it's useful for you to know the different ways that authors might receive this. For example, if you know that the author has already received feedback from beta readers, you can ask them what the readers thought of the book – which could help you with your analysis.

Alternatively, you might be approached by an author whose budget doesn't stretch to a developmental edit. If they haven't heard of beta reading, you can suggest this to them as another option.

3 | General principles

Because there is so much scope in what a developmental edit can include, it's important to keep a few key principles in mind. This way, you can be sure that you're doing a good job and providing the most value to your client.

Remember, it's not your book!

Always keep in the forefront of your mind that the book you are working on isn't your own. Your task isn't to rewrite the book to your own preferences, or turn it into something you might have written. Instead, it is to encourage the author to make their book the best *they* can make it.

To do this, you'll need to ask the author about their creative goals so you can determine what they're trying to achieve. You'll still need to bring some of your own creative thinking to the table, though. After all, novel-writing is inherently creative, and problems relating to creativity require creative solutions.

By understanding the principles of good writing and being empathetic to the author's vision, you can help the author develop their book in their own way.

Avoid overwhelming the author

By communicating with the author and reading their manuscript, you'll be able to get a sense of their abilities. Be sure that your recommendations are appropriate to the author's skill level, otherwise you could overwhelm them to the point that they're unable to effectively implement your feedback.

It can also be useful to include only a handful of the most impactful suggestions in your feedback. If you try to get the author to address every single tiny issue, not only do you end up providing reams of feedback – which would take you a long time to write – but the author might end up focusing on the smaller, easier changes and not on the harder, bigger and more impactful ones.

If necessary, you can suggest the author make one set of changes and then submit their revised manuscript for a second round of feedback.

Provide objective feedback

Strive to be as objective as possible with your feedback. A personal opinion on a book isn't as valuable as an objective analysis. To help an author make their book suitable for their target readership, think about how the book will appeal to a large number of readers – rather than just you, a single reader. Developmental editors do this through providing considered analysis rather than emotion-based opinion.

For example, 'I don't like the main character' is opinion, and not one that every reader might share. If you dig a little deeper into why you don't like the character, you might find it is rooted in subjectivity – for example, perhaps they remind you of someone you dislike.

Feedback such as 'The main character's tendency to complain all the time makes them quite unsympathetic' is more analytical – not only have you identified the reason for your dislike but you have also explained it in a way that is more objective.

This is not to say you can't be emotional in your feedback – it's impossible not to have an emotional reaction to a book! Instead, you can use those emotions to inform your analysis.

Understand novel-writing conventions

It's important to root developmental analysis in theory rather than personal ideologies or preferences. When it comes down to it, there are no rules in fiction due to its inherent creativity – but there are conventions. Conventions are expectations: readers will have certain ones when they pick up a book, even if they aren't aware of them – and when these are fulfilled, they feel satisfied.

For example, it's a genre convention that in a tragedy, the main character will make an error that leads to their death (usually a literal death, sometimes a metaphorical one). Think of any of Shakespeare's tragedies (*Macbeth*, *Othello* …), but also novels such as *Things Fall Apart* by Chinua Achebe, or *The Kite Runner* by Khaled Hosseini.

A more general writing convention that readers expect is that the main character introduced in the first part of the book will be the character which the rest of the story follows.

However, a book needs to contain a balance between originality and convention. If something is too conventional, it can be quite boring; if it goes too far the other way and is overly unique, it can be difficult to read and enjoy. Often, manuscripts fail because they are not subverting convention *effectively*: this usually happens due to the author's lack of understanding of convention, or lack of technique (or imagination).

Continuing the example above: an author who doesn't understand general writing conventions might start their novel focused on one character, then get bored of writing about them and switch their focus to another. The result is a disjointed and unsatisfying reading experience.

However, George RR Martin subverts this exact convention when he introduces us to Ned Stark at the beginning of his epic fantasy series, *A Song of Ice and Fire*, then kills him off at the end of the first book. Martin's series follows another convention of epic fantasy, which is that there can be multiple main characters, and so killing one isn't detrimental to the reading experience because the reader has other characters to carry them through the story.

The subversion of one convention is therefore supported by the inclusion of another. By killing off a main character early in his story, Martin subverts the convention that a main character introduced early in a story should still play a large and active role throughout the rest of the story. This makes readers aware that no character in Martin's story is safe (even if they are a main character). The author turns convention on its head, but skilfully and with purpose.

Developmental editors can help authors understand whether they are failing to use effective conventions or subverting conventions ineffectively, and advise them how to fix this.

> **The author turns convention on its head, but skilfully and with purpose.**

4 | Writing-craft topics that you need to know about

As we've established, there are many components that go into a novel, and developmental editors need a good understanding of these to form the basis of their analyses. It's one thing to instinctively know that something isn't working in a story, but developmental editors need to be able to pinpoint exactly what is going wrong and why so they can advise their clients with authority and provide effective feedback.

The deeper your understanding of what makes a novel work, the more nuanced and useful your analyses and suggestions can be. You will be able to explain your suggestions to an author, and this in turn will enable them to revise with confidence and understanding.

This chapter gives you a flavour of the kinds of topic you need to know about to be a developmental editor. There is a lot to learn about each one, but much of it is beyond the scope of a short introductory guide, so further reading has been provided in the **Resources** at the end of this guide.

Story

In essence, story is the amalgamation of the connected events depicted in the manuscript. A story must have a beginning, middle and end – and there should be significant change through each of these stages. Events should be connected by cause and effect, the sum of these parts working together to create a narrative whole. Developmental editors analyse the story to see if it fits together in a logical and satisfying way.

In addition, the whole story needs to be compelling. Compelling stories raise interesting questions about what's going to happen (or has happened). These are narrative 'hooks' – they make readers want to continue reading to satisfy their curiosity. Compelling stories also contain plenty of conflict (from minor, such as a character talking to another in a condescending way, to major, such as a character deciding whether to shoot a home intruder). If the main character gets what they want without opposition, there is no story. Conflict drives change – and change lies at the heart of all good stories.

Story structure forms a large part of literary analysis and theory, and it's useful to study the prevalent ideas in this area to help with your analyses. As a minimum, developmental editors would be well served by a solid understanding of narrative arc and the three-act structure. This is a simple framework that shows how plot points (story events) connect to create a satisfying story. There are other effective frameworks, but this is the most common.

Basic narrative arc

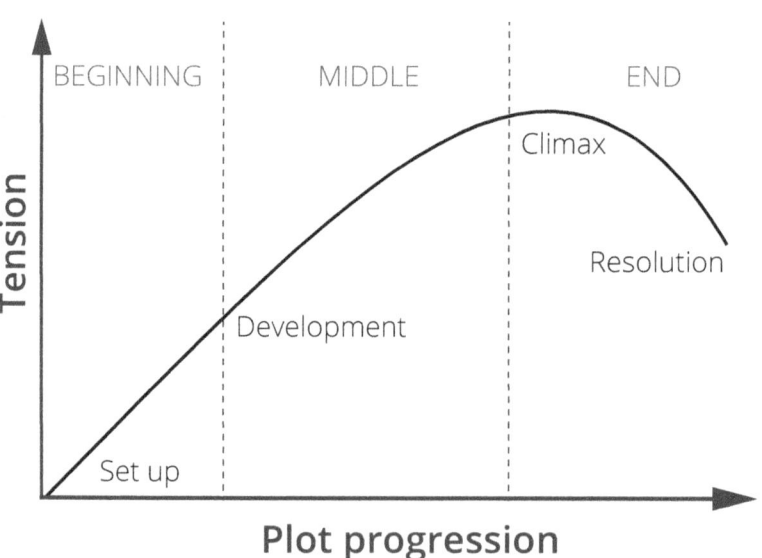

Figure 1 The narrative arc is created when tension is plotted against plot progression on a graph.

> *Questions to ask yourself*
> - Does the story hang together – does it have a beginning, middle and end linked by cause and effect?
> - Is there significant change happening throughout the story?
> - Is the story interesting – are there enough narrative hooks, and does it contain enough conflict?
> - Are there any problems with plausibility or major plot holes – are there errors or inconsistencies in the story that go against its established logic?

Plot

The plot is the selection and ordering of the connected events of a story. An effective plot is put together in a way that reveals a novel's dramatic, thematic and emotional significance. Plot is the *design* of the story, although many people use the terms 'plot' and 'story' interchangeably. Generally, this doesn't matter, as long as it's clear what is being discussed.

A story might be plotted chronologically, or jump forward and backward in time, or one thread might be put down for a while for another to develop. Some events might be skipped over completely (and happen 'off the page'), while others might be explored in detail.

Developmental editors need to consider whether authors have chosen the most significant events of their stories and ordered them in the most effective way. They might suggest that some events are cut from the story, while others are added and/or placed elsewhere.

> *Questions to ask yourself*
> - Does the manuscript start and end in the most impactful places?
> - Are flashbacks well positioned?
> - Are events ordered in the most meaningful and effective way?
> - Are there any superfluous events that could be cut?
> - Are the story threads balanced in a way that keeps readers engaged?

Character

Characters are the people (or animals or entities) in the story who bring about the plot. Generally, the reader will be rooting for the main character due to the very fact that it's their story they are following.

Some stories have more than one main character. Some will have two (often telling the same story from two points of view), while others have multiple main characters (for example, epic fantasy novels tend to follow many characters across multiple, interconnected story threads).

There is a lot for developmental editors to assess when it comes to character. Interesting characters have agency and are not just swept along by events (although it is possible that they'll start out passive, so that their character can develop). The protagonist should make decisions that move the story forward: in this way, character and story are closely connected. What a character wants and experiences influences the decisions they make, which in turn power the story.

Characters don't necessarily have to be likeable, but they do need to be interesting. If a novel is mostly plot-driven (that is, the events of the story are engaging enough to carry a reader's interest through to the end), the author might not need to have particularly deep characters. However, completely 'flat' characters are extremely boring to read about! Instead, authors should try to make their main characters 'round' – in other words, give them depth and make them feel real.

Developmental editors can advise authors on how to do this through techniques such as:

- putting more of the character's inner life on the page
- giving them meaningful backstories
- having them express deep and complex emotions
- giving them interesting and unique world views, etc.

> *Questions to ask yourself*
> - Who is the main character (or characters), and what makes this their story?
> - Is the main character interesting, and do they feel real?
> - Do the characters have sufficient motivation to drive them through the story?
> - How do the characters develop and change?
> - Are there any less important characters that aren't needed in the story?

Point of view

Point of view (POV) describes where the lens through which the reader experiences the events of the book is placed. More often than not, we experience the events of a novel through viewpoint characters. This means the sensory details, thoughts and emotions depicted in the book are experienced through a particular character.

It's easier for authors to write and control one viewpoint character per chapter or section. When events and experiences are filtered through multiple characters in a single scene, readers can lose their connection with the main viewpoint character, and the narrative can feel ungrounded and confusing. If the POV moves very quickly from one character's experience to another, this is known as 'head-hopping' and is best avoided.

A narrative written from an 'omniscient' viewpoint can share multiple characters' POV, but this style of narration is difficult to execute well (and has fallen out of fashion in many genres of contemporary commercial fiction). This is not to say it shouldn't be used at all, just that it requires more understanding and carefully controlled technique.

Table 1: POV description and book examples

First person
A character tells the story from their own perspective. In singular first person, the pronoun 'I' is used. Though uncommon, plural first person is also an option, where the pronoun 'we' is used.
Unless the character is telepathic, they can only express the events of the novel from their own perspective and have knowledge of things only they have experienced.
If they learn things from other characters, this knowledge is filtered through (and potentially distorted by) their interpretation.
The Hunger Games by Suzanne Collins *The Handmaid's Tale* by Margaret Atwood *My Sister, the Serial Killer* by Oyinkan Braithwaite *Eleanor Oliphant is Completely Fine* by Gail Honeyman
Second person
The narrator is either a character who refers to themselves as 'you' to distance themselves from the events, or a separate entity trying to assimilate the reader into the story to create a sense of intimacy and, potentially, surrealism.
Second-person narration is difficult to pull off and not a very popular mode, although it is occasionally used in experimental literary fiction.
If On a Winter's Night a Traveller by Italo Calvino *A Prayer for the Dying* by Stewart O'Nan *Halting State* by Charles Stross *Bright Lights, Big City* by Jay McInerney

4 | Writing-craft topics that you need to know about

Third person

There are many factions of third-person POV, but its defining feature is that all characters are referred to by he/she/it/they (or any other third-person personal pronoun).

Third-person limited (or subjective) roots the perspective firmly in the viewpoint character, whereas third-person objective places the lens outside the character, so that events are more observed than experienced.

How close or far the lens is to the experience of the character is known as 'narrative (or psychic) distance'.

> *Under the Skin by Michel Faber*
> *Normal People by Sally Rooney*
> *Over My Dead Body by Jeffrey Archer*
> *Harry Potter and the Deathly Hallows by JK Rowling*

Omniscient

The narrator knows everything and isn't limited to the viewpoint of any single character. An omniscient narration could be written in the present or past tense and use first, second or third person.

The narrator could be a character in the story (such as a god or enlightened person) or an observing nonentity.

> *The Hitchhiker's Guide to the Galaxy by Douglas Adams*
> *The Book Thief by Markus Zusak*
> *The Vanishing Half by Brit Bennett*
> *Dune by Frank Herbert*

Developmental editors consider whether the author has written their novel using the most effective POV, and whether that can be improved. POV affects how close readers can feel to a character and how much information they have access to, which in turn can influence tension, pace and writing style. The POV an author chooses has huge ramifications on the reading experience, so it needs careful thought.

Narrative style is the culmination of several decisions an author has made about how they are telling their story. This includes whether they're using first-, second- or third-person narration, plus the tense they have written in (past tense is the most common, although some authors write in the present tense; the future tense is extremely rare and experimental), plus the chosen viewpoint.

> *Questions to ask yourself*
> - What viewpoint is being used, and does it work with this story?
> - Is it handled with consistency and logic?
> - If multiple viewpoints are being used, are the transitions between them clear and smooth?
> - Is the narrative (psychic) distance handled smoothly and effectively?

Setting and worldbuilding

The overall setting of a novel includes the general location and historic time (for example, Tudor England or an interstellar society in the distant future). Each scene in the novel unfolds in a more specific setting (for example, the banquet room of a castle or the desert plains of a specific planet).

Setting isn't just the stage on which characters act; the setting itself can provide conflict and challenges, and can create mood and set the tone for the unfolding action. Authors should consider their setting as much as any other aspect of their novel.

Setting is a part of worldbuilding. Even authors who set their story in the real world must do some level of worldbuilding – whether that's inventing a room in a house or selecting details of a real-world city to help create tone, mood and theme. For authors writing about the real world, worldbuilding is about rebuilding the world on the page with design and purpose.

Worldbuilding is particularly important if the author is inventing their story world (or part of it) from scratch. It's a huge part of science fiction and fantasy, and setting is only one piece of this puzzle. Everything – from how physics work, the environment and the culture of the people who inhabit the world – interconnects.

> *Questions to ask yourself*
> - Does the setting feel vivid and real?
> - Are the details correct for the time period?
> - Does it feel as though the action is unfolding in the right place, or would somewhere else provide better dramatic opportunities?
> - Are there inconsistencies or anything illogical about how the invented world works?
> - Are details or setting and worldbuilding seamlessly woven into the narrative, or do long passages of unnecessary exposition stop the flow of the story?

Scene and summary: show and tell

Authors need to decide what aspects of the story to 'show' the reader and what aspects to 'tell' them. They need to balance how much of the story unfolds before us and how much is explained to us. In general, a novel should consist of a series of scenes interspersed with small amounts of narrative summary (which either links scenes together, or is embedded within them).

Scenes are passages in which characters interact with each other or their environment in a way that feels like events are unfolding in real time: think of them as the *dramatisation* of the story. Narrative summary describes events in a way that doesn't feel as though they are unfolding in real time.

'The gravel crunched underfoot as she made her way down the drive, and she whistled to herself before nonchalantly rapping on the front door' is an example of a sentence you might find in a scene, whereas 'She went to Clare's house for dinner before meeting Tim for drinks later in the evening' would be narrative summary.

One of the main uses of narrative summary is to reshape time: events are skipped over or condensed, or time is paused to give characters space for introspection. Narrative summary can also contain explanation and information, which is a form of *exposition* (information that comes from outside the current viewpoint to give readers additional context or information).

If there is too much narrative summary in a novel, it can slow the pace of the story and make readers feel disconnected from events and characters. Developmental editors keep an eye on whether too much of the story is being told and not enough is being shown through effective scene writing. They can also advise an author when events can be summarised if they don't effectively serve the plot, which can help to increase the pace.

> *Questions to ask yourself*
> - Is there so much narrative summary that you feel you are being told the story rather than experiencing it?
> - Are there any boring or unimpactful scenes that would be better summarised and condensed?
> - Does every scene serve a purpose in moving the plot forward or deepening characterisation or theme?
> - Are the scenes immersive and interesting?

Genre

Genre is essentially a category of composition that takes into account technique, tone and content. It's useful for developmental editors to understand the genre in which the author is writing (for example, romance, fantasy, science fiction, horror, etc) so they can best advise them on whether their manuscript is likely to adequately satisfy the genre's readers.

We can think of genre as a set of conventions and codes shared via a kind of implicit contract between reader and writer. For example, a convention of the romance genre is that the story has a happy ending with the two romantic leads together, while a convention of the horror genre is that there is often a false ending, where the main character thinks they've overcome the threat before it re-emerges for the true, final showdown. Being well-read in a particular genre will give you a sense of its conventions.

Readers come to a piece of writing with certain expectations (conscious or otherwise), and these are either satisfied or subverted – but an author needs to understand these expectations for either of these things to happen effectively.

Having said that, a good story is a good story, regardless of genre – and genre conventions are often less of a consideration than everything else we've talked about in this guide when it comes to helping authors develop their novels.

Questions to ask yourself
- Have genre conventions been used to good effect?
- Are any important conventions missing?
- Could any subversions be more effective?

Readership and market potential

Developmental editors sometimes provide their clients with an analysis of how well a novel might sell in the marketplace – or its potential to sell, once the editor's advice has been implemented. However, not all developmental editors offer this as part of their service. Some simply focus on helping the author elevate the general quality and readability of their book, without going into any detail about market trends and potential readerships.

It's useful to keep in mind that whether a manuscript is of 'publishable quality' or whether it has a good chance of selling are two different things. To be of publishable quality, the manuscript must contain a coherently written story that other people are likely to enjoy – but this doesn't necessarily mean it will sell well.

It can be difficult to judge whether a manuscript has good sales potential. Different genres have differently sized readerships with different reading habits, for example. But knowing what readers want to read is tricky, and you'll need up-to-date knowledge of the book trade to make some informed guesses here.

Keep a finger on the pulse by browsing bookstores, attending publishing events, reading new releases in your genres, and subscribing to magazines and blogs in the book industry. Ultimately, no one can really predict whether a book will sell once it's published.

Why might authors need to consider this? Self-publishing authors might need to forecast their sales potential to work out a sensible budget for publishing their book. Agents and publishers want to sign books that sell well, so authors hoping to go down this route need to consider whether their book has enough sales potential to be of commercial interest, and how this could be improved, if needed.

It can also be useful for authors to think about what publishing success means to them. Are they more interested in winning literary prizes, or do they want to earn as much money as possible? Developmental editors can give authors a sense of their book's potential without crushing their dreams or giving them false hope – and advise them on how they can better reach their goals in this area.

Questions to ask yourself
- Who is this book for?
- What kind of readers will it appeal to?
- Have similar books been published?
- How successful have similar published books been?
- Are there any major aspects of the story or writing style that might prevent the author from achieving their publishing goal?

5 | Conducting a developmental edit

In the previous chapter, we looked at several different craft elements that go into writing a novel that developmental editors need to know about. But how do you put that theory into practice? How do you communicate your observations and suggestions with the author?

As mentioned previously, developmental editors each conduct their service a little differently from one another. There is really no right or wrong way to do things, but generally, most developmental editors present their feedback as an editorial report and/or as notes in the manuscript pages themselves, so that's what we are going to look at in this section.

Different approaches to feedback

Some editors dive straight into providing feedback on the page without having read the manuscript first. The benefit of this approach is that the author sees how a fresh reader might experience their novel. However, reading the manuscript first in its entirety arguably enables you to provide a deeper and more nuanced edit, because you can help the author shape their story with knowledge of how each part works together. You can also better advise the author on creating effective foreshadowing (that is, hints at what's to come later in the story that create suspense), and cutting or reducing anything less important or superfluous to the story.

One feedback round

Some editors provide only one round of feedback.

They might provide:

- only the editorial report
- only notes on the pages
- an editorial report and page notes in tandem.

Any of these methods can be effective, but keep in mind that if you need to suggest big changes to the manuscript, there is a chance that extensive page notes could go to waste. For this reason, think carefully about your method, and make sure it is effective. For example, you might decide not to provide detailed feedback on the pages you recommend the author delete, or you might provide extensive feedback on a single chapter (instead of the whole book) to demonstrate how the author can express their story through scenes instead of narrative summary, with the recommendation they rewrite much of their manuscript using what they've learned from your detailed notes.

More feedback rounds

Other editors provide two (or more) rounds of feedback, with the author revising the manuscript between those. This method can be extremely effective in helping the author elevate their draft – but it can also be costly for the client, and time-consuming for both of you.

An example of this method might be that the editor provides general feedback in the form of an editorial report, the author revises their manuscript, then the editor provides detailed page notes on the revised draft. The greatest benefit of this method is that the author has a chance to fix any manuscript-wide issues so that very few (if any) page notes go to waste, and the editor's suggestions can provide a deeper level of feedback than would have been previously possible.

Factors affecting approach

Approaches to developmental editing are dictated by various factors:

- The editor's preferred way of working – they might decide to offer their service using a fixed method.

- The current state of the manuscript – the further it is away from publishable quality, the more extensive and in-depth the editor's feedback needs to be.
- The client's creative and publishing goals – for example, perhaps they only want feedback on how the story hangs together, in which case an editorial report focusing on this aspect alone could be suitable.
- The client's time and budget restraints – these impact on the kind and depth of feedback an editor can provide.

Whatever the approach, it should be agreed on upfront with the client, along with the fee (or your estimated fee, depending on your pricing method) and timeline.

Gathering information

The first step of every developmental editing project is information-gathering. The client contacts you, asking if you can help them with their manuscript. Before you say 'Yes', you need to make sure this is indeed the case!

Some editors gather this information through email exchange, a phone or video call consultation, or by sending the client a questionnaire they have created for this purpose.

Questions to ask

Here are some questions you might ask the client. As you gain experience, you can tailor this process to your individual needs and include more questions.

- What is the title of the manuscript?
- Is it a complete draft?
- What is the word count?
- What is the genre?
- What age is the intended audience – adult, young adult, middle grade, etc?
- Are there any trigger warnings or sensitive content?
- What are your publishing goals?

- What are your creative goals?
- What do you hope to achieve by working with me?
- Are there any deadlines for this project?

Also ask to see a short synopsis (summary of the plot) that includes what happens in the beginning, middle and end of the novel.

Some developmental editors prefer not to know the outcome of the story before they start working on the manuscript, so they can gauge their reactions as a reader. If you'd prefer to work this way, ask the author to share the concept of their story instead of their synopsis. This should cover the story goal, the conflicts that the protagonist faces and the stakes (what will happen if the protagonist doesn't achieve their goal).

As well as a synopsis or concept, ask to see a sample of the writing – preferably the whole manuscript.

Reserve the right to decline

Keep in mind that you have every right to refuse projects if you don't feel they would be a good fit for you. That might mean:

- your services are not a good match for the client's needs
- the manuscript is written in a genre you aren't familiar with, or don't like – and so you wouldn't feel creatively connected to it
- the manuscript contains content you find upsetting or distasteful.

For example, some editors do not work with erotic fiction or horror, or stories that contain sexual abuse. Your mental health is important, so don't feel bad for turning down work on these grounds.

Assessing and pricing projects

Once you've conducted your information-gathering, it's time to assess and price the project.

If your client is a publisher or packager, they are likely to have a budget and schedule in mind, and should be able to brief you on what they want. However, if you are working directly with authors, be mindful that their needs, budgets and schedules will vary. Many authors are unfamiliar with editorial processes and terminology, so they might not know what service they need when they first approach you – especially if you offer multiple services.

For this reason, it's important to take some time looking at the manuscript sample and the synopsis or concept before you agree to work on the book.

Select sample pages to read

Reading the opening chapter and a few pages from the middle of the manuscript should give you not only an idea of how refined the writing is, but also whether there are any obvious issues relating to technique. Is the POV clear? Is the balance of scene and narrative summary well considered? And so on. The more issues you spot during a cursory look through the materials, the more work the manuscript is going to need.

Looking at the synopsis or concept also helps you assess whether there are greater issues with the broadest aspects of the novel:

- Is the idea compelling?
- Does the story have a clear beginning, middle and end? (This is easier to determine by looking at a synopsis.)
- Is there a main character driving the story?
- Is there sufficient conflict and change?

Try to gauge whether the story hangs together as a whole, or whether the author needs specific help in developing their concept and/or plot.

Decide how to price

How a developmental editor prices their service depends on a huge number of variables and preferences. Some editors provide a predetermined service for a specific fee (often based on word count), while others provide a tailored service and fee based on the estimated amount of work they think the project will entail. Neither method is more correct than the other – it just depends on how you want to run your business!

Why sample edits are problematic

Many sentence-level editors provide sample edits. These can be extremely useful in:

- helping convince clients of the value of an editorial service
- ensuring both parties understand the scope of the service
- helping editors determine how much work might be involved in the edit or proofread – which in turn helps them prepare their quote.

However, it can be difficult to give sample edits as a developmental editor. This is because a developmental editor needs to take a big-picture view of the manuscript (in relation to the author's creative and publishing goals) and this is hard to do without a lot of work upfront.

If the developmental editor conducts their service by writing summary letters and doesn't provide page-specific feedback, this can be difficult to demonstrate on a smaller scale. For this reason, many developmental editors do not offer sample edits. Some do provide detailed creative feedback on a few pages, with the caveat that a full developmental edit takes into account the manuscript as a whole.

(For more in-depth discussion on this topic, refer to the CIEP guide *Pricing a Project: How to prepare a professional quotation* by Melanie Thompson.)

Page notes

When a developmental editor goes through the manuscript file page by page, they don't edit in the traditional sense. Instead of making substantial changes to the text itself, they make suggestions on where and how storytelling techniques can be strengthened.

The number of comments and suggestions a developmental editor provides on manuscript pages can vary greatly. Some manuscripts require more suggestions than others if there are a lot of issues to address, but it's also down to the editor's personal working style. For example, as noted earlier, some editors want to address as many issues as possible on every page, whereas others might decide to focus on fewer issues and address one at a time, so as not to overwhelm the author.

However, this isn't to say that no direct edits are ever made to the manuscript during a developmental edit. Some developmental editors *do* make direct changes – editing to demonstrate fixes to the big-picture issues they've spotted, such as how to deepen the POV. Other editors still might label themselves as developmental editors, but their service falls on the substantive, line-editing end of the scale: they make lots of direct edits to the text and focus less on how the author might make more general novel-wide revisions.

As determined at the start of this guide, the definition of developmental editing varies greatly – and how an editor interacts directly with the manuscript is one of the biggest variables.

Editorial reports/summary letters

An editorial report or summary letter (also known as an 'editorial letter') is a document summarising your assessment of the author's manuscript and your main suggestions on what they can change to improve it so it has a better chance of achieving their creative and publishing goals.

Once again, the length and depth of these letters vary greatly between editors. Whether you write your editorial report first and then use it to guide your page notes, or make notes on the pages first and then summarise these in your report, depends on what makes most sense to you and your method.

Constructing a report template

Many developmental editors find that using a template to structure their editorial report is extremely useful. The editor creates a document with headings, notes and possibly template text to help them structure their feedback logically and make sure they don't forget to include certain points.

The template (and ultimately, the report) is broken down into sections based on the storytelling techniques and principles discussed earlier in this guide: for example, story, character, POV, etc. Used conscientiously, a template won't make your feedback formulaic, but it will save you time and effort.

Selecting the topics to report

Don't feel you need to address every topic in the template you create. You can add or remove topics to suit the needs of the manuscript or the parameters of your service. To reiterate a main principle discussed earlier in this guide: be careful not to overwhelm the author. Perhaps, for example, there are no major issues with POV in the manuscript you are working on, so your feedback praises the author on doing this well and then focuses on other areas which can be improved.

Make your editorial letter as clear and digestible as possible. The use of headings helps here, but you can also use bullet points, tables and even graphs to help illustrate your points.

Pointers on providing feedback
Introduce the report and balance the comment

It's a nice idea to provide an introduction in your summary letter: this usually includes an explanation of how your feedback is going to work, and your main impressions of the manuscript.

Making sure you acknowledge the manuscript's strengths is important here, too. Receiving criticism can be emotionally difficult, and although you want to focus your report on what the author can do to their manuscript to improve it, remember to include plenty of praise so you don't inadvertently make the author feel inadequate as a writer.

Avoid assuming the author knows what they've done well. If they can't see where the novel needs improvement, they also might not be able to see where they are succeeding.

Sign off positively

Closing paragraphs (or conclusions) are equally important. The author has just been alerted to some of the ways their writing is not working – and sometimes this will be in more ways than they've anticipated – so you want to leave them feeling encouraged and motivated rather than deflated and defeated.

This is also a good place to briefly summarise the main ways you think the manuscript can be improved so the author doesn't feel overwhelmed with all the changes they might need to make to their book.

Use a feedback framework

When writing your feedback, consider using this framework devised by developmental editor and tutor Jennifer Lawler:[1]

1. **Identify the problem**. State the problem clearly, so the author knows what it is that needs to be addressed.
2. **Explain why this is a problem**. Describe the effect the issue is currently having on the manuscript.
3. **Suggest a solution**. Give the author a general idea of what they might want to do to fix the issue. Consider providing a specific suggestion for illustrative purposes, while making it clear that your idea is one possible way to address the problem.

Here is an example of how this might look in practice:

> There is a subplot in which [name of secondary character] deals with and recovers from a serious illness. [**Identify**]
>
> This subplot does not link to the main plot or the themes of the novel, and though the experience changes the character, these changes have no bearing on the story. Because of this, it feels disconnected from the rest of the novel and causes the main story to come to a standstill while the subplot takes place, negatively affecting the pace. [**Explain**]
>
> Consider cutting this subplot from the novel so that readers can be swept along more easily by the compelling main story. [**Suggest**]

---
[1] Club Ed: clubedfreelancers.com

Be sensitive

Do write your feedback with authority, but ensure your tone isn't berating or condescending. Always remember: there is a person at the other end of your comments and you are trying to help them, not demonstrate your superior knowledge.

At the same time, avoid writing in too timid a tone or one that's overly complimentary for fear of hurting the author's feelings. It would be unfair for them to believe their novel is better than it is because of your feedback, and then receive a multitude of agent rejections or bad reviews.

Focus your analysis on the manuscript, not the author. For example, 'The character development needs more work' feels less of an attack than 'You need to work on your character development'. Above all, make sure your tone is kind.

Book maps and summary spreadsheets

A book map or a summary spreadsheet is essentially a breakdown of a manuscript into its component scenes and chapters. There are multiple ways to create and present a book map, but a simple table is one of the easiest.

There are a number of potential options here:

- The author might have already created their own book map, and you can ask to see this.
- You can ask the author to create a book map and submit it, along with their manuscript, for review.
- You can create a book map to help with your analysis – which you may or may not hand over to the author.
- You might not use a book map at all – it's simply a potential tool.

Each row of the table contains a short summary of each scene as the novel progresses, and columns can include additional information such as word count, viewpoint character, time and setting. A book map provides a broad overview of both the structure and plot of the manuscript, which can help greatly when analysing these components.

6 | Next steps in becoming a developmental editor

We have covered a lot of practicalities in this guide – and as you have seen, there is a lot to know about what makes good fiction – but the number one thing that makes anyone a good developmental fiction editor is being truly and deeply interested in reading novels. By reading voraciously, you subconsciously absorb many lessons in what makes a good novel – and what makes a bad one! By reading analytically (that is, with additional awareness and consideration), you deepen your understanding further.

Read widely – and if you want to specialise in editing a particular genre, make sure you have read the classics in that genre, as well as a lot of contemporary novels. This gives you a thorough understanding of how the genre works, as well as what readers enjoy in today's market.

Learning and training

It isn't quite enough to read a lot, though. You also need frameworks on which to hang your understandings, and language through which to discuss your observations and thoughts. That's where reading literary criticism and books on writing craft come in.

To learn the practical skills involved in developmental editing, and to get a better sense of how all this writing-craft knowledge might apply to novels-in-progress (that is, not the final iteration of a piece of writing in its published form), it's useful to learn from other developmental editors. This can be done in several ways, from taking courses (perhaps the most streamlined and focused method), to formal and informal mentoring (for example, talking to other editors in online forums or in person).

Building experience

Just like any other skill, your developmental editing skills will get better the more you use them. You might decide to work for free on a manuscript or two, just to find your feet and gain that valuable first bit of experience, or to practise privately on published novels. (You'll probably find you have more to say about novels that have been poorly reviewed!)

You could also consider offering beta reading as a way to dip your toes into providing big-picture feedback. As mentioned previously, this kind of feedback is more opinion-based than analytical.

You don't have to know everything about writing-craft theory straightaway. You simply need to know enough to help authors improve their manuscripts – because improvement, not perfection, is the aim. Moreover, the more you learn, the more issues you might be tempted to try to help the author fix, but remember to avoid causing overwhelm. You still need to determine what changes will have the biggest impact on a novel, and that is its own separate skill.

The more manuscripts you work on, the more you might see the same issues cropping up, and the more confident you will feel in guiding authors on how to address these issues. However, one of the greatest pleasures (and challenges) of developmental fiction editing is that every manuscript is different: there are multiple ways to view and address issues. As a developmental fiction editor, you will find yourself continually challenged in fresh ways.

Many authors will be extremely grateful for the developmental guidance you give them. If you go on to read subsequent drafts of the manuscript, or see the book in its final published form, there is nothing more satisfying than seeing that an author has taken up your advice and redrafted their book to better reach its potential.

7 | Resources

Courses

Liminal Pages (run by Sophie Playle, the author of this guide) offers several comprehensive on-demand and tutored courses covering the foundations of writing-craft theory, and the practical side of offering developmental editing: **liminalpages.com/courses**

Club Ed (run by Jennifer Lawler) offers many on-demand and tutored courses covering specific aspects of developmental editing: **clubedfreelancers.com**

The EFA often runs tutored courses (tiered by experience level), as well as the occasional webinar related to developmental editing: **the-efa.org/active-courses**

The CIEP offers an introductory course to fiction editing that focuses on copyediting but covers some ground regarding writing-craft theory relevant to developmental editing: **ciep.uk/training/choose-a-course/introduction-to-fiction-editing**

Books

Books are an excellent resource, not just for you but also for the authors with whom you work. It can be very useful to point authors towards books that address their manuscript's specific areas of weakness, so they can learn more.

Publishing and editing
- *An Editor's Guide to Working with Authors* by Barbara Sjoholm
- *Creative Self-Publishing: ALLi's guide to independent publishing for authors and poets* by Orna A Ross

- *Self-Editing for Fiction Writers: How to edit yourself into print* by Renni Browne and David King
- *Self-Editing for Self-Publishers: Incorporating a style guide for fiction* by Richard Bradburn
- *Write to be Published* by Nicola Morgan
- *Writers' & Artists' Guide to Getting Published: Essential advice for aspiring authors* by Alysoun Owen
- *Writing a Marketable Book: A seriously useful author's guide* by Charlie Wilson

General writing craft
- *How Fiction Works* by James Wood
- *Into the Woods: How stories work and why we tell them* by John Yorke
- *Literary Analysis: The basics* by Celena Kusch
- *Monkeys with Typewriters: How to write fiction and unlock the secret power of stories* by Scarlett Thomas
- *Poetics* by Aristotle
- *Reading Like a Writer: A guide for people who love books and those who want to write them* by Francine Prose
- *The Magic of Fiction: Crafting words into story* by Beth Hill
- *Writing Fiction for Dummies* by Randy Ingermanson

Specific writing craft
- *Creating Characters: The complete guide to populating your fiction* by The Editors of Writer's Digest
- *Description and Setting: Techniques and exercises for crafting a believable world of people, places and events* by Ron Rozelle
- *Dialogue: Techniques and exercises for crafting effective dialogue* by Gloria Kempton
- *Elements of Fiction Writing – Characters & Viewpoint: Proven advice and timeless techniques for creating compelling characters* by Orson Scott Card
- *Elements of Fiction Writing: Scene & structure* by Jack M Bickham
- *Fixing Your Character and Point of View Problems: Revising your novel* by Janice Hardy

- *Make a Scene: Crafting a powerful story one scene at a time* by Jordan E Rosenfeld
- *Nail Your Novel: Writing characters who'll keep readers captivated* by Roz Morris
- *On Dialogue* by David Bohm
- *Plot Versus Character: A balanced approach to writing great fiction* by Jeff Gerke
- *Point of View: How to use the different POV types, avoid head-hopping, and choose the best point of view for your book* by Sandra Gerth
- *Save the Cat! Writes a novel* by Jessica Brody
- *Sin and Syntax: How to craft wicked good prose* by Constance Hale
- *Story Engineering: Character development, story concept, scene construction* by Larry Brooks
- *Technique of the Drama: An exposition of dramatic composition and art* by Gustav Freytag
- *The Emotional Craft of Fiction: How to write the story beneath the surface* by Donald Maas
- *The Hero with a Thousand Faces* by Joseph Campbell
- *The Power of Point of View: Make your story come to life* by Alicia Rasley
- *The Science of Writing Characters: Using psychology to create compelling fictional characters* by Kira-Anne Pelican
- *Wonderbook: The illustrated guide to creating imaginative fiction* by Jeff Vandermeer
- *Writing Voice: The complete guide to creating a presence on the page and engaging readers* by The Editors of Writer's Digest
- *Writing Your Story's Theme: The writer's guide to plotting stories that matter* by KM Weiland

Blogs and websites

Andrew Wille: **wille.org** (lots of free resources and astute insights into the world of publishing).

Emma Darwin: 'This Itch of Writing': **emmadarwin.typepad.com/thisitchofwriting** (clear and insightful writing advice on a range of topics).

Jane Friedman: janefriedman.com/blog (lots of writing advice but especially useful for publishing advice).

KM Weiland: helpingwritersbecomeauthors.com (especially good advice regarding structure and character).

Liminal Pages: liminalpages.com/blog (articles about professional developmental editing, as well as writing-craft advice).

Roz Morris, 'Nail Your Novel': nailyournovel.wordpress.com (especially good for literary fiction craft advice).

The Bookseller: thebookseller.com (business intelligence and analysis for the book trade).

Writer Unboxed: writerunboxed.com (huge number of articles on the art and business of fiction).

Forums and communities

CIEP Fiction Special Interest Group (SIG) chats in the official CIEP sub-forum and hosts regular themed Zoom discussions.

Fiction Editors of Earth Facebook group: facebook.com/groups/883454338368110

The Editors Lair is a forum that contains a subgroup for fiction editors: editorslair.com

About the author

Sophie Playle is a professional fiction editor who also teaches online courses to other editors. Speculative and literary fiction are her favourite genres to edit, and she loves working with authors who are passionate about high-quality storytelling.

Sophie is an Advanced Professional Member of the Chartered Institute of Editing and Proofreading, and has an MA in Creative Writing from Royal Holloway, University of London.

liminalpages.com

Acknowledgements

Thank you to everyone at the CIEP who worked on this guide, and special thanks to Graham Clarke and Rachel Rowlands for their reviews. Thanks also to Jennifer Lawler for permission to quote her three-step feedback framework.

www.ingramcontent.com/pod-product-compliance
Lightning Source LLC
Chambersburg PA
CBHW041311110526
44590CB00028B/4327